EIVED

09 2018

IEW LIBRARY

NO LONGER PROPERTY OF
SEATTLE PUBLIC LIBRARY

The Law of the
    Unforeseen

Copyright © 2018, Edward Harkness
All Rights Reserved

ISBN 978-0-912887-71-5

Library of Congress Control Number
2018938190

Front and back cover art: Doris Harkness
Design: Lauren Grosskopf & Ed Harkness

Pleasure Boat Studio books are available through your favorite bookstore
and through the following:
SPD (Small Press Distribution) 800-869-7553
Baker & Taylor 800-775-1100
Ingram 615-793-5000
amazon.com and bn.com

and through
PLEASURE BOAT STUDIO: A LITERARY PRESS
www.pleasureboatstudio.com
Seattle, Washington

Contact Lauren Grosskopf, Publisher
Email: Pleasboatpublishing@gmail.com

Also by Edward Harkness

Saying the Necessary
Beautiful Passing Lives
Ice Children, a chapbook
Syringa in Twilight, a chapbook
Watercolor Painting of a Bamboo Rake, a chapbook
Fiddle Wrapped in a Gunnysack, a chapbook

NO LONGER PROPERTY OF
SEATTLE PUBLIC LIBRARY

The Law of the Unforeseen

Poems by

Edward Harkness

PLEASURE BOAT STUDIO:
A LITERARY PRESS

CONTENTS

For Linda, Devin and Ned Harkness,
for my mother, Doris Harkness,
and in memory my father, Harry Harkness (1925-2010)

BLANK PAGE

Face it. You're locked in a barless cage.
Each way out goes back in,
like a Möbius strip or Escher staircase.

It's only paper, after all, a planless
floor plan, a plane not quite spatial,
not exactly a hotel room in Rome

where something surprising might occur—
a meeting, say, with a tour guide
who will explain in the lilting music

of an Italian accent your itinerary
through the city's ancient streets.
She'll point out ruins, bazaars along the Tiber,

lovers at night dangling their ankles
in Trevi Fountain, and then treat you
to a glass of local red at a table

in Campo de' Fiori, there to hear
the bells from distant St. Peter's,
to watch the throngs of tourists,

to study the night sky. Far better this
than to stand in line by yourself
on the slippery Italian marble floor

of the blank page, its empty cathedral
echoing all the things you might have said
to break the silence of your life.

You're not in Rome any more. You're home,
starting from scratch, pacing again
the corridors of the blank page,

imagining a chair, a table, a vase of cosmos
inviting you to sit, to consider how small
the universe is, how simple, how patiently

it waits for you to add to it—whatever
you care to add—stars, waterfalls,
the names of those you loved, those

you didn't love enough. Even the blank
page belongs on the blank page,
always empty, always full of promise.

One: Great Apes at the Zoo

Oh, when they heard that Louis was dead,
All the people, they dressed in red.
The angels laid him away.

~From the song "Louis Collins," by Mississippi John Hurt

THREE ITALIAN PRUNES

roll off my desk at work, and of course
I must ponder this inconsequential event,

as if adhering to it grants it eternal life,
and damn, they're bruised and bleeding now

in my hand. I look at them as Newton did
his famous apple, also bruised, no doubt,

but a bruise that led to the glue of the universe,
a world that pulls us toward its heart,

which is good and bad, good in that
we don't float through life as anemones do

in the starless deeps. Bad in that we're magnetized,
tethered to the three dimensions,

always feeling about for the fourth or fifth
key ring to the beyond. I pick a scab

of purple prune skin from my teeth.
In truth, there are no dimensions.

There's merely now, my cluttered desk
with its pens and sandwich wrappers,

and an 1886 edition of Berens' *Hand-Book*
of Mythology: Myths and Legends of Greece and Rome,

in remarkably good condition considering its age,
owned once upon a time by a young scholar.

On the inside cover she has floridly fountain-penned
her name, Amelia, notes she's 17, boarding

at something-or-other academy in Charleston.
She likes Athene, has scrawled "Athene" here and twice

on the secret back inside cover. Amelia has,
I discover, underlined a passage: "Pallas-Athene,

goddess of Wisdom and Armed Resistance....
is the only divinity whose authority was equal

to that of her father, Zeus himself."
As for the prunes, I ate them, they were delicious,

so sweet and so cold. As for Berens, he writes
with the clarity of the stream into which Narcissus gazed.

As for Amelia, her secret is an open book.
She's fallen hard for the goddess of Wisdom

and Armed Resistance, the two of them
now married to the scintillant dust of eternity.

~ With apologies to WC Williams and EM Behrens

8

COMING TO TERMS WITH THE FACT THAT I MAY NEVER GET THE HANG OF MISSISSIPPI JOHN HURT'S "MONDAY MORNING BLUES"

I said it and life goes on.
It's not just the complicated 6/8 time,
or the continuous alternating bass.
And it's not the smooth-as-a-baby's-butt
slides from the 3rd fret to the 5th,
and the instantaneous requirement
of the left-hand fingers that they leap
from the barred A-chord to the 5th fret D,
or the two-step dance of the right thumb
thumping the thick baritone E-string,
or even the jump back to A and a rather
eccentric little duet you do
with your left pinky and ring finger
to make an A-sharp major diminished,
or whatever in God's name Hurt does there
to resolve the dissonance and settle back
into the barred A. Nor would I say
it's the slurring of certain notes,
the hammer-offs and hammer-ons
scattered variously throughout the ragged
bluesy but up-tempo wizardry on the 1965
recording I have, now so scratched
as to be almost unplayable. And it's not as if
my no-longer-nimble fingers
refuse to hop and skip gymnastically
up and down the fret board, as they once did.

It's the damn song—that's what trips me.
It's the blues of Monday morning,
you feel around for your shoes—gone—
and you realize you're in jail,
you don't know why, nobody does—
in jail, you realize, for six long weeks today,
so goes the song. Tomorrow's your trial day.
What might be my fine, you're wondering.
Can't be too much, can it?
Then the trial, you've played the song
over and over, nobody cares how many hours
you've put in, you yourself don't care,
you just like to play, but the jury says guilty,
the judge says *Get a pick and shovel,*
let's go down in the mine. That's the only time,
that's the only time, that's the only time,
you ever felt like crying. Mister,
change a dollar and give me a lucky dime.
Jail or mine—there's no escape, none,
except by playing again and again
Hurt's simple, wickedly difficult tune
with your forever tender fingertips
raw from pressing the steel wires—
except by singing your way,
no matter how badly,
through the secret air duct of music.

CLEARING BRUSH

I'd fallen asleep in the snow. Waking,
a thin coverlet slid off my poncho.

There lay the handle of my machete,
long as my forearm, its dented blue blade

already stained with rust, blade and forearm
put to the test that winter to clear brush.

I rose and re-entered my sodden life,
the one I'd just left, the one on a bluff

above the beach where on clear days you'd see
the blue Olympic Range across the Sound.

If the tide was slack, the Sound flat as glass,
you'd see, far out, the dark backs of orcas

rise and fall, the blades of their dorsal fins
knifing through the swells. No clear view that day.

No mountains. All horizons hemmed by snow,
a wet smattering on the boughs of firs

and alders along the cliff
of seldom-visited Alder Park.

Our job: to whack scotch broom, a buck an hour,
paid in cash by a cadaverous park

supervisor, Basil, who never spoke,
merely nodded and appeared not to breathe.

My workmate, Walter—aka "Waltzer"—
McCann, claimed title to a Cadillac,

a decrepit thing, once green, now the grey
of waste-water. An oily knotted rope

held the passenger door forever closed.
No window. In the predawn he'd honk twice,

beckon me to *crawl* in, a 5-minute
endeavor, lunch bucket first, then to hunch

on a mush of newspapers that did not
well cover the seat springs. He'd creep

the long way to the park, as if giving
a guided tour of cheap motels, car lots,

mini-marts along Aurora, always
taking the detour to pass Golden View

Cemetery, rolling down his window
to call out "Good morning, darling"

to Delores, his wife, asleep among maples.
Six hours a day we'd swing our machetes,

the blades ringing when they bit the wrist-sized
trunks of broom and dogwood. By March,

we'd slashed and piled a mountain of brush
just as snow began to fall, lacing our ugly heap

into a thing of delicate beauty.
After lunch, shoulder squealing, I lay next

to the pile, using a red bandanna to shield
my eyes from the pricks of wet snow.

The nap was a white cradle of silence,
broken by the Cadillac's throaty growl.

I never understood why we were there,
Waltzer and me, clearing the bluff of brush.

Brushing off my poncho, blinking away
the icy splats, all I knew is that I'd been reborn—

not into the radiance of paradise,
but close enough—a white newness

to everything, a cloud of blue exhaust,
a furious choir of sparrows from within our pile,

and the rattling emphysemic rasp of Waltzer McCann
calling to me to clamber through the window,

asking would I be so kind as to spot him a Big Mac,
large fries and Diet Coke on the way home.

CATCHING THE VASE

Twice now, reaching for something—a light switch
that first time—you've caught the ceramic
Chinese vase before it went to pieces. This morning,

your sleeve snagged the lid stem just enough
to cause the vase to teeter and topple
off the end table. You dove in a way

you didn't know your body could move
except during sex. Your heart became
an instant rose, your head struck the edge

of the table, your foot kicked out like a third
hand clawing at the throat of death, caught the vase
soccer-style with a socked instep and held it

for the quarter-second your hands needed
to make the grab. You averted that disaster,
bandaged your forehead and noticed once again

the three goats painted on the urn's globed face—
one white, one black, one brown—all three browsing
beneath a leafy tree. You always thought the urn

an ungainly melon, hardly pristine,
its rim chipped, the lid broken and repaired—
less antiquity and more thrift store—

very likely a water jar, neither rare
nor old, or, that is, not old for the broad river
of Chinese history, or the broader river

of its pottery. Late Qing Dynasty, maybe,
early eighteen hundred-something, bought
on the cheap at a "ghost market" in Tianjin.

Still, you love those ugly goats, the misshapen tree,
and the plum-colored sun perched oddly
in one of its limbs. You saved the day this time.

The third time, all charms will end. The goats
will turn to shards on the hardwood floor.
You picture yourself sweeping, grieving,

sifting the remains into a trash bag.
Your eyes lie, seeing things not there, not seeing
things that are, not seeing the goats as homely,

funny, frolicking like real goats,
not seeing the plum sun as precisely placed
by the artisan, not seeing the scarred

lopsided tree as a Daoist poke
at Confucian harmony, and only now
seeing for the first time the stream

sluicing down a hinted-at hill from behind
and to the right of the tree, curlicues of water
curling over hinted-at rocks in calm blue curves.

The stream has no source. The black goat,
leaf in mouth, studies you with an animal's bland
curiosity. There'll be no third lucky catch. One day,

you—or someone—will dive and miss. You love
the goats because they're there, because the plum sun
climbs the limb forever, or at least for now.

AMERICA, GREAT ONCE AGAIN

Riot cops have slammed the woman with green streaks
in her dark hair onto the airport's marble floor.
I count eight from the posted video, whose eye peeks
blinking between protesters near a glass door.
She sobs, cries out, "Stop! You're hurting me!"
The eye moves to show a girl's head. She's ten,
I'd guess. Cornrows, hands over ears—that's all I see,
all I need to see, must always see—men
in body armor, one boot on the woman's back,
one on her neck, while others tie her wrists,
twisting them till she shrieks, her body slack
from writhing against what it resists.
The recorder, as her video blurs and ends,
whispers in her phone, *We're so fucked, my friends.*

SCENE ALONG THE DRIVE

"Make money, stay sane." Richard Hugo, from "Glen Uig"

Some afternoons my eye will stray
from the work before me—
a form to fill, a bill to pay—

as now, to a young gray squirrel
frisking in the dirt along the drive.
He approaches a stick, his tail

upright, a flag of caution,
as if the stick might be a snake.
And in a sudden blur of motion

he bites it and flips it in the air,
then tumbles in the gravel, crazed
with what outwardly might seem fear

but is, to my human eye, play, nothing less.
He disappears into a laurel hedge,
returns to the stick to toss

once more his toy, and again
he leaps up, as if possessed
by the smoke of dust, then gone.

And I wonder if, to stay alive,
I must make believe, must lie—this event,
for instance—in order to revive

myself, always gasping, near to drowning
in the rising sea of America.
Everyone's got a gun, and they're aiming.

They'll never know the secret joy
of imagining the scene I see—
squirrel, stick—whatever it might be—

that invents the world to the world.
The mind—mine—must be allowed to stray
to keep the rising tide at bay.

GREAT APES AT THE ZOO

Behind the glass barrier and the laughter
of children and parents, the mother sits,
eating something the keepers have given her.
She holds a rind—avocado or papaya—
as if it were a small ceramic bowl,
lifting morsels of whatever it is to her mouth.
She delicately licks her slender fingers.
Squatting in straw, she seems Buddha-calm,
unaware of the gawking world,
unaware, too, apparently, of her tussling boys,
one no bigger than the toddler beside me,
his nose to the glass, squealing in recognition,
as if he too would like to wrestle and box.
The straw flies. Dust rises in misty puffs.
The little ape slaps his older brother,
does a back flip, bumps his head on a log,
runs to mama, and crawls on her back
to catch his breath. Mama doesn't budge.
She drops the rind and surveys her world
of leafless climbing trees the keepers have installed,
a webbing of ropes, an artificial stream,
and across it the dark pocket of a concrete cave.
Her eyes are bland, resigned,
like the eyes of any prisoner or refugee.
Kids and their parents have strolled away.
The older brother shits in the straw,
then knuckle-walks to the stream
where he cups his hands to drink.

The mother gazes off, as if at some other life.
She reaches back and lifts her little fellow
over her head, rolls sideways onto the straw
and grooms him till he falls asleep.

Two: The Gods

"They all go ice-free in the future."

-Comment by Marika Holland, a senior scientist at the National Center for Atmospheric Research in Boulder, Colorado, regarding the predictions of her computer models that track the rapid disappearance of ice in the Arctic Sea. (From "Does the Disappearance of Sea Ice Matter?" by Jon Gertner, *New York Times Magazine*, July 29, 2016).

ICE CHILDREN OF THE ANDES

Priests led the boy and girl up the steep trace
above their village wedged in stone
and stunted pines. Small plants brightened the slope,
their red leaves frost-whitened in mid-day sun.
The young ones had been well-fed, dressed
in buckskin chewed to soft felt. Both wore beads
of azure and shell, their feet fur-shod
against the raw uncaring stones.
Below, gorges flowed with lakes of mist.

Now and then they paused to rest, the priests
speaking in solemn tones, pointing out
the silver of distant rivers, torrents veined
in the creased walls across the chasm.
They asked the children if they could hear
the mountains call to them to climb on.

And when in the thinning air the girl and boy
could walk no more, the priests bore them
on their backs, arriving in twilight
at the ice cave, its opening scalloped
to a glass polish, its blue ceiling
catching the last light exhaled by the gods.

They sat them down, fed them coca leaves
to put their fears to sleep. The priests addressed
the gods, describing the girl's head tilted
on her shoulder. The boy, they reported,

remained upright, his frozen hair laced
across his glazed eyes, his lips parted
as if on the verge of speech, as if to tell his sister
his dream, how he fell into a warm river,
how he swam until it spilled him into the sky.

ICEBERGS NEAR TWILLINGATE

From this bluff on the coast of Newfoundland,
hulks appear like a ghostly armada.
Near one, a sight-seeing ship vanishes
as it passes behind a steepled mass—
a sudden lesson in size, scale, distance
and the shape of things to come.
Bergs, I learn, wander a mile a week,
bearing cargoes of blue light.
Notre Dames of ice, their buttresses crack,
spires break, topple, un-architected
by the warming Atlantic.
I picture myself on a pier
when one of the bergs arrives,
awash, smaller than a dinghy, en route
to nothingness, a glass gargoyle, last one
of its kind, bobbing next to a piling.

TO THE WOMAN AT THE MARCH

She was frail, bespectacled, in a dated
but flowery housedress, light
for the warmth of the day. Her hat,
too, seemed to come from another era,

likewise bedecked with flowers—
small, needle-pointed rosebuds, I believe
they were. Me, white. She, black.
We had marched together with the others,

some thousands, neither of us speaking,
turning now and then to smile as if
to acknowledge that we were, both of us,
alone, thrown together by chance,

hemmed by the river of our fellows
flowing salmon-like to the rhythm of someone
drumming, someone playing a recorder,
another far ahead exhorting us

with a bullhorn to chant in unison
our anger, our conviction—*The people,
united, will never be defeated.*
The march ended at a park where,

more or less unscripted, our throng formed
a great choir before the makeshift stage,
to await the dozen speakers gathered
with their prepared sermons.

Somewhere from behind rose
the hymn "We Shall Overcome."
That's when, without looking, she took
my hand, squeezed it not gently,

and joined in. I felt her bright contralto
first as a hum, so pure it frightened me,
its current rising through my wrist,
up my arm, where it settled in my chest.

And I, who cannot carry a tune to save
my life, sang *Oh, deep in my heart,
I do believe, we shall overcome some day,*
wishing as I sang never to let go.

HONEYMOON

A delirium of blossoms, he recalled.
Here we are on the bank of the Huzo,
walking in pink snow.

They were Americans, in love with love,
spellbound by pictures of Mount Fuji
they'd seen in *National Geographic.*
And there it was, appearing at sunrise
on the train window. *How about that,*
he'd said, waking her. *It seems to hover.*
It's a vision, a floating island,
a perfect cone, just like the photos—
so symmetrical, so ideal, darling, like you.

In Kyoto, the river glided,
bright as mica, tinged with glacial till.
All the city, it seemed, had come to savor
the soft explosions of cherry trees,
just as they had come, these newlyweds,
arriving in a rickshaw, crowding with others
onto boats poled by young men
whose tanned arms glistened in April sun.

Then, excursions to temples and gardens,
where the azaleas had just begun to ignite
among the Zen stones. *Such tranquility,*
he told her on a stroll. *Such harmony*
with the natural world, don't you think?

You won't find that back home.
They even made love in a bamboo grove,
he remembered, thinking at the time
they were alone, with only the calls
of the different birds high in the green light,

then noticing as she rolled off him onto the moss,
her skirt askew, they were being watched.
An old woman in a conical hat smiled.
They smiled, mortified, unable to answer
the woman's slight bow and greeting: *Konnichiwa.*

So long ago it was, that afternoon in the city
of pagodas and monuments, markets thronged
and rich with smells they'd never smelled.

*Now, for Christ's sake, they want to try out
the new bomb—Fat Boy, or Fat Man, or something—
on Kyoto, our Kyoto, where we climbed above the river
to that temple. What was it called?* She wept, even,
when statues of the Buddha would appear
as if by magic, like sudden awakenings, among the pines.

He could imagine the shrines flattened,
ancient timbers blown to kindling by the blast,
the curved black roof tiles of ten-thousand buildings
swirling in typhoons of white fire.

Our city, for God's sake. Our city.

Even the ice-fed Huzo would boil,
its boats aflame by the collapsed bridge
they'd walked across a dozen times,
and the young men who poled the boats—
they'd be burned to death in seconds.

So charmed the couple had been, so taken
by the politeness of the bowing Japanese,
so delighted were they when,
pulling their phrasebooks from their rucksacks,
they'd stutter a few words to a shopkeeper
or a woman planting rice shoots
along a road, and be understood.

He would demand that the committee
remove Kyoto from the list of targets.
Surely there were other cities more suitable
from a military standpoint,
more appropriate strategically.
What about Kokura's munitions plants?
What about Yokohama or Hiroshima?
No matter what General X said or what General Y
argued would be the Emperor's next move,
no matter what logic or tactical line of thinking
they'd array on their table of maps,
damage projections, casualty estimates,
he'd hold the line. He would not stand by
to see Kyoto—their Kyoto—
reduced to miles of radioactive ash.

The bomb, he vowed, would be dropped,
just not on the city he loved, his Kyoto.
His decision would be final.
Was he or was he not Secretary of War?
He'd go to Truman, if necessary,
get the full backing of the President.
Not one Shinto shrine, goddamn it.
Not one Zen pavilion. Not one pond of koi,
not one boy—I see him plain as day—
little canvas knapsack on his back,
riding his rickety bike to school,
pausing on the bridge to cover his ears
against the howl of air raid sirens.
I see him turn for home at the instant
the sun comes down to earth, flowering
like God knows what—a rose, a death rose
of heat and fire. No, no and no.
Not in Kyoto. Not in our Kyoto.
They'll have to add another city to the list.

[Author's note: Henry L. Stimson (1867-1950,) US Secretary of War, 1940-1945, was de facto head of the Manhattan Project. This poem is loosely based on an event from Stimson's life.]

THE GODS

They sit on comfy thrones and drift through time
high atop their Hawaiian Islands in heaven.
They snack on manna and nectar, those famous

unworldly hors d'oeuvres, and watch in mild
curiosity as we cross ice bridges and deserts.
They see us lashed to make-shift rafts,

tossed on oceans, amused by the prospect
that there's just no way we'll make it,
that we'll topple, eventually, off the rim

of the earth. On occasion they're diverted
by the rise and fall of our empires.
They smile and roll their eyes

at the puny attempts by some of us to appear
almighty, by this or that poseur who ends at last
as a shriveled mummy inside a pyramid.

That's good for a chuckle. The gods take more interest
in our wars, recent or laced with the dust of history.
To the gods, the Trojan War was yesterday.

Like ageless toddlers, their attention span
is limited. Immortality can be tedious. After all,
they must appoint countless ministers to run

countless celestial agencies, not to mention
the hundred thousand jugglers
whose job it is to keep the cosmos in motion—

precisely why the gods barely give us
the time of day, why they fail to notice us in an unused
closet of one of their million winter palaces.

They save their affections for new-born stars.
As grandparents, they fawn over galaxies
we'll never learn of, far beyond our little chips of glass.

Of course they have a soft spot for their
pet nebulae, and watch them with delight
as they flare in the fire of spectrums and halos

we'll never observe, no matter how long we wiggle
through the eons, morphing a little here and there,
nothing to write home about. To the gods,

we're an anomaly, a quirk among
the infinite number of possible constructs.
It's all relative to them. There's so much

they must attend to: the mountains and continents
of eternity, the fabulous geometry of matterlessness,
the great towers built out of heat

and the spliced guy wires of space and time—
all those gravity-sucking vampires who must be watched.
It's demanding work, being a god, but not without

the occasional down time and wild parties. You'd think
we'd be modeled in their images and not the other way
around, as is the case. We're barely a second thought.

What intrigues the gods, however, are the rivers
of silver—newly discovered—said to flow on Io,
a moon of Jupiter. That, they find, is exciting.

THERE'S NOTHING LEFT TO SAY

There's nothing left to say
about the earth, about the day.
Who will bail us out
now that God has about
had it with his fun?
There's nothing under the sun,
new or old. No one sings. No one.

Why do mountains drown?
No one dreamed we'd crown
a blind man, mute as well.
He sneered and locked us up in hell.
Now the seas have risen.
There's nothing under the sun,
old or new. No one sings. No one.

The garden of dead cars,
their missing eyes eye the stars.
Where will children play?
All the songbirds have flown away,
following rivers that never run.
There's nothing under the sun,
old or new. No one sings. No one.

THE HOUSE OF MYSTERY

We stood in the deeps of redwood shade just off 101, the nearly-
forgotten Pacific Coast Highway—a break from our family trip
and the long haul to L.A. Mom paid the man in a cowboy hat

a dollar. Over there, said the man, pointing to a wood porch
and small door. We shuffled down a dim hall, floorboards wincing,
rotted in places, rat turds scattered like black rice. My younger brother,

not ten feet up the narrow hall, now loomed huge, two heads taller
than me. There was my proof of unseen forces.
Through glassless window frames, redwoods tipped at crazy angles.

Some older boys in the house shoved each other, banged
into plywood walls and laughed. A sign warned something like:
Below this house, geologists have discovered a massive asteroid

known to be taller than the Eiffel Tower. This asteroid, said the sign,
has powerful but as yet unknown properties. Parents, please
supervise your children at all times. Don't let them out of your sight!

Around a dim U-turn, another sign with a red arrow
warned that visitors in the House of Mystery should
not attempt to open the Yellow Door, padlocked for our safety.

A family from France, said the sign, had gone through
the Yellow Door and were never seen again. We four—
Dad, Mom, my brother and I—paused before the Yellow Door.

A faint strip of gold light shone from below. I felt an icy draft
on my ankles. That's as far as we got in the House of Mystery.
Back in the car, my head still whirled. I'd felt the dizziness,

the vague nausea caused, I was certain, by the hidden power.
Even at 14 I had my doubts about everything. I believed in ESP,
poltergeists, the inexplicable. I believed in the asteroid,

the magnetism that caused trees to lean sideways.
How else explain the dizziness, the difficulty of walking
upright, the urge I felt to fall on my face? How else

explain the chill seeping from under the yellow door?
What of the French family, who might have taken the warning
for a joke and gone through, never to return?

And what of the band of light? How I'd have loved to open
the Yellow Door, to see with my own eyes the source
of that gold glow, to feel the pull of the hidden power.

"BARB'S HEALING HANDS"

"Barb's Healing Hands," says the hand-painted sign
I pass each day on my neighborhood stroll.
Who's Barb? There's her hand-lettered phone number
in black. Those would be her hands, I gather,
pressed not quite in prayer, more like reaching—

a little swollen, the fingers crooked,
arthritic on a plywood stand propped up
on curbside grass. Apparently, Barb does not
paint well. The bouquet of florid lilacs
the hands hold, faded by the usual

erasure of sun, rain and winter wind,
seems childlike, as if she'd turned the pages
of Gardner's *Art Through the Ages*, pausing
at Gauguin, her brush daubed in Prussian blue.
I could use Barb's healing hands myself.

The world could. Every day the unspeakable occurs
somewhere, in some far country, some city,
prison, senate chamber, *my* city, *my*
neighborhood. Every blessed day Regan
gouges out Glouster's eyes. Soldiers fire missiles

through the windows of a family's bedroom.
I should drop in some afternoon and see
what Barb charges, assuming she still lives,
assuming Barb's Healing Hands still massage
those muscles knotted from living on earth.

Her hands might revive my numb lower back,
my bum left shoulder. As for the world's aches,
Barb would need, like Maioshan, Chinese goddess
of mercy—she who hears the cries of the wretched—
every one of Maioshan's one thousand healing hands.

Three: Ash

I was fifteen, I think. Wilmington then
was far along on its way to becoming a city
and already well-advanced on its way back to dust.

~Galway Kinnell, from "Memory of Wilmington," in *Mortal Acts, Mortal Words.*

THE RETURN

The name of my grandmother's horse
escapes me, as most names do, finally,
cantering into the trees of unremembrance.

Any number of times she would tell
of a blond girl crouched over the pommel,
the saddle's horn bumping her sternum,

her hair flying, slapping her neck,
clods and dandelions leaping as she streaked—
Streak! Yes! That's the name she gave

to her chestnut filly, its forelock blazed
with a lightning bolt—as she streaked
across her father's orchard, ducking limbs

of cherry and pear, where now a freeway
overpass curves high into a cloudless day,
shading me in the din of traffic

hidden overhead as if a waterfall
might be near, or an airport runway
and not this vacant parking lot,

its asphalt littered with plastic trash,
broken by dandelions outside an abandoned
tanning salon where the orchard might have been.

PHOTO OF THE TWINS, CA. 1897

For the pose, they pinned white camellias
in their hair, so despite the dark heavy gowns,
it would have to be April in Indiana.
They are the Savoy girls, Mert and Gert.
Mother Amanda stands between, her small
mouth so pinched she appears to want to spit.
Maybe she's annoyed by the endless wait
for the photographer to light his white powder,
a flash that will briefly blind her
and propel their faces toward the future,
to this kitchen counter, where now they gaze
at me as if they've never seen a clean-
shaved man in some kind of billed woolen cap
festooned with the letter S. They're aghast.

The photographer wanted symmetry. Thus,
Mertie's hair topples left, Gertie's right.
They'd have been something near 18.
All the evidence—the ruffled sleeves
of their gowns, the girls' several rings, tresses
in pleated waves toppled nearly to their knees,
Amanda's gold time piece half-mooned
from her waist pocket—points to late 1890s,
hardly gay if judged by their somber eyes.
So demure the girls are, so dear, so
unsmilingly radiant, as though they've glimpsed
a forecast of the century about to dawn.

No names on the back of the photo.
Mert could be Gert, for all I know.
The one on the right is the prettier,
softer, though more forlorn. I can't release
my gaze from theirs. So unsettlingly direct
are their eyes, they seem outside of time.
That, and the strict formality of the pose,
suggests this studio photo was their debut
to the world, and the world, if I rightly read
their looks, is cold—something the twins feel
but can't explain—not yet, not at 18.
Maybe I read too much. Maybe the photo
merely reflects its era—the time of taffeta,
bustles, bowlers and steam trains, before
the invention of the photographic grin.

Or maybe I know too much. Know, for instance,
of Gertie's failed marriages, her moves
from Evansville to Bremerton to Pasadena,
her job there as a maid in a rich man's home.
Mertie, I learn from an early city directory,
lists her occupation as "laundress." So the photo
shows them staring at the blank wall of their future,
and the future is a blinding flash of light.
Their expressions are intricate—accusatory
but not unsympathetic, as if, somehow, they see me,
well aware that I've looked too long and deep
into their hearts, dwelled too long in the ill-lit
rooms of their lives, and thus learned things
they themselves, beforehand, could not have fathomed.

Do eyes forgive? Let that be true as the camellias
behind their ears. I want to think my kinswomen,
Mert and Gert, would smile, finally, or at least
have understood—not forgiven but understood—
my life's work, which has been to rouse them,
raise them from their graves, to light the flash
that saves them, and saves the unsmiling
radiant world, against all odds, from oblivion.

DAHLIAS

Endless replication of clam shells, ants,
hyacinths in spring, the return of Orion,
the floral design of pond ice—things never stop.
You stand by her stone and picture

how she rolled her hair in that tight silver bun.
You see her on her knees among gaudy dahlias,
tanned arms dirt-flecked, neck sweat-beaded.
Silver strands come loose, quick-swiped back

behind her ear—scenes you play over and over
because they're yours, because the sky is pale.
You divide yourself between all-is-illusion
and who-the-hell-cares. She ran off with a man,

Archibald something, Wyoming, 1920-something,
she 19 with child in tow—your father, as it happens.
You only knew her later—her silver hair,
freckles under her green-specked eyes.

In loving memory, intones the stone—stock phrase
if there ever was one. Still, it's true, if complicated.
The squabbling robins in the laurel hedge agree.
So does April drizzle. Those dahlias were as colored

as her life, just as real as your love for her.
Real too is your father's life, written in the Book
of Sorrows Unspoken. The world recycles itself,
breaking your heart and, somehow, mending it.

BLUE HYDRANGEA

With apologies to Rainer Maria Rilke

When she returns from the store,
I'll tell her I've written a haiku for her,

for the blue of a blue hydrangea.
I lie, as she will immediately know,

about writing a haiku. I'll tell her
it's no longer possible to write

any kind of poem about hydrangeas,
haiku or otherwise, not after Rilke,

who likens them to strange notepaper,
unlike the yellow legal pad

that suffers my failure to see the blue
in this mass of petals arranged in a vase

on the kitchen table. The petals are soft
green coins, washed-out gray-green

some might see as a kind of almost-blue,
hazy like dusk, like memory,

the undiscovered blue of time,
the blue of childhood sadness,

scribbled on strange notepaper on which
I've written the longest haiku in history:

July already?
Hydrangea petals—mintage
of a winter sky.

When she sees the vase of hydrangeas,
when I read to her my bad haiku,

she'll know I've adhered to Basho's dictum:
"Learn the rules, then forget them."

She'll know that beauty happens sometimes
by surprise, like summer stars gone to seed,

like the coin of a sudden moon on the window,
its almost-blue smudged on the hardwood table

by the vase of hydrangeas no longer blue
but the color of the night sky.

A X

1.
The new-honed ax he swings freezes mid-stroke
in a photo never taken. You could
walk up to him. You could peer into his
gray eyes, examine his peppery beard,
his grimed, care-lined brow, sweat bright on his neck,
muscles tensed, veins bulged, ready for duty,
eager to relax but ready. You could
study the hunks of green pine—a small pile
since he's just begun to split fifty rounds
on this fall morning behind the mess tent
where the reek of rancid bacon fills his head.

He looks familiar, this living statue,
far from County Antrim, now just outside
of Murfreesboro, Tennessee. Well he should.
He smelled the bodies an hour before
he saw them, arrayed in rows neatly near
the rail line, most, but not all, blanketed.
So goddamned young, he thought, like George,
his son, somewhere in the Kentucky hills,
traipsing with the cold, exhausted 13th Illinois.

2.
As it must, the ax head flashes downward,
hard, glancing off the slick bark of the round.
Again you stop the frame to consider
the fate of your great grandfather's grandfather,
this lean weaver who lied when he enlisted,

said forty when the truth was fifty-five.
By now he'd heard too much the din of war—
the clatter of caissons, the snort and shit
of horses, the silence and sudden shrieks
of limbless men, their curses so appalling,
so loud he more than once had covered his ears.

His sergeant, a Maine man not yet twenty,
had barked, *You, private. Two cords. Do you hear,
Irish? Go, man!,* then tossed the hickory-
handled ax on the ground. Several pickets
galloped by, their horses seething. One yelled
Nashville! Action in Nashville, you fresh fish!

3.
The ax head skids off the edge of the round,
slices through the leather of his brogans,
embeds itself well into his right foot
between the big and second toe, some four
inches in, severing bone and tendons,
ending, for him, the Civil War three months
from that morning he volunteered.

You think of what he might have had inscribed
on his stone when, in Anderson County,
Kansas, 1884, still hobbled,
having outlived three of four children,
he died in a dusty town called Lincoln.
He could have had *Into the bosom of Christ*
chiseled into the granite, or such like.
Or nothing more than his Scots-Irish name

and dates to encompass a mere arc of time.
The top of the stone broke off long ago.
It leans against the base so that Thomas
is no longer joined to Harkness. The sum
of his life thus reads: "He was a soldier
in the Union Army." The sum of his life.

Why that? Surely this sojourner must have
wondered what he'd got himself into,
here in America, roaming from upstate
New York, there to marry Eliza, then
on to the textile mills in Queens, and by
1855 a shoemaker in Illinois,
now here at rest in Centerville,
next to Margaret, his surviving daughter.
The ax has gone to rust, just as his stone
will fall away to pieces, chunks, gravel, grit,
and at last to dust, its inscription
reduced to a whisper in the elms.

POTATOES

He came to me on one of those mild,
late winter days, my gloved hands gripped
on a hoe handle handed down from someone—
Aunt Philomena, it might have been,
or Ted Strickler, both gardeners, both gone.
Sweating, I'd flung my jacket on a limb
of the plum tree, went on breaking clods
with the nicked hoe blade until I was stopped
by the odor of cinnamon and pine.
I'd backed into the rosemary bush,
releasing its tang, releasing too my father.
He appeared as he had in his last year—
cheeks papery, ashen, eyes dull, thin scruff
of beard no longer white but yellow.
He told me he was okay, said I needn't worry
or feel sorry. And just as when he lived,
having lost by then his sense of taste and smell,
he laughed, went on and on about how much
he loved my potato wedges—salted, roasted
with rosemary, daubed lavishly, as always,
despite my frown, with mayonnaise.

MY FATHER MOWS THE LAWN

Slacks rolled, tee-shirt speckled green,
sweat-stained in the heat of July,
he'd push the mower through the knee-high grass.
Thankless task, after a day at his cubicle,
now home to the rectangle we called our yard.
I offered to help. *Nah,* he said. *Exercise.*
I'd hear him curse when the blade
cracked against a rock or bit into an object
hidden and rotting in the weeds.

Again I see him crouch, extract from the reel
a wet black thing twined in dandelions.
Without a word he chucks it high
into the summer afternoon. I watch it spin,
shedding bits of earth, flapping like a wounded crow.
When I catch the chewed, un-seamed baseball,
he claps his hands, dances around the mower
and whoops, *What a grab in deep left field!*
We go to extra innings. This game is tied!

I toss back the ball. He's turned away already,
straining, muttering, wrestling the mower's wooden
handles like a man who's had it, who knows futility
and puts his whole being into its resistance.

TYING A TIE

I must be twelve or so. We face the bathroom mirror,
me in starched white shirt, trying not to squirm,
faint frown on my face. He in sleeveless tee,
his chest hair abundant, still dark, the last dots

of shaving soap on his chin. He calls the knot a Windsor,
holds my hands holding the long end on the left,
short end on the right, flipping long over short,
looped around, poked up and over the top

tucked in, pulled down, the triangle tightened
with thumb and forefinger—all simple, deft,
impossible to replicate. He's not a sad man yet.
I'm in training for the world, for being a man like him,

sad only when I study him in the mirror,
girding for another day at the appliance store,
his hands on the shoulders of his smaller self,
prepping me first so I can see how it's done,

how to tie the tie in a way that allows me to breathe,
to not fear the squeeze of being choked.
I will, just as he has, come to live with it.
And so I have, now that he's gone, come to live

with it, to tie my own tie, to accept the discomfort
just as he did, whose reasons for sorrow were many,
to love again the appliance salesman who turns me
to face him as he adjusts the knot at my throat.

ROOT BEER FLOAT

There will come a time when, up at some ungodly hour,
you pull from the freezer compartment the quart of vanilla,

well-expired by now, its contents iced-over, slightly yellowed.
You pry out two decent scoops into the tall blue-tinted glass,

drop to your knees, fish behind the pickle jar in the fridge
to find the one bottle of root beer, still there from the picnic in July.

You pour it down the side of the glass, watch the foam rise
over the ice cream, seething toward the rim, certain to spill.

It does not spill. First you lick the froth, a speck of it
cool on your nose. Your mother, a soda jerk as a newlywed,

introduced you to the fine art of the root beer float.
Your father, having survived the war, favored cherry sodas

with a "bird heart"—so he called the maraschino marble—
bobbing in the bubbles. He sold appliances, a business that failed

after a year. For each customer who bought a refrigerator—
so she told you years after he died of AIDS—

he'd stuff the refrigerator freezer box with TV dinners
and a quart of vanilla ice cream. Ice cream, root beer—

you regard it as wondrous as the teachings of the Buddha.
Still, there will come a time when you spoon out the last

white blob, slug back the last of the root beer, rinse the glass,
then search for and find the special ball point pen

you'd been looking for, blue like the glass, with Vincent Van Gogh
on the clip, a trinket someone sent from Amsterdam, and

at that ungodly hour you drift back to the page you've been avoiding,
the one you were working on with its dozen or so

inconsequential lines about your first job out of high school
as a cook on a fishing boat in Alaska, how lonely you felt,

gazing out the tiny galley window at the gray sea, the immensity
of distant mountains, how happy you were when the skipper

fired your ass because you could not cook your way
out of a paper bag, because the crew of four bearded men were—

so to speak—fed up, half-joked they'd sneak down
to the engine room where you slept in the fo'c's'le, slept,

even as the engine thundered all night, half-joked they'd bind you
in your hammock and toss you over the side into the cold

blackness of the Gulf of Alaska. There will come a time.
It's all inconsequential froth in a tinted glass, fizzing up,

subsiding like your maunderings, like that mixture
of sassafras and vanilla, how it drinks up ten or so icy minutes

of your life. There will come a time when you open
the fridge and find it empty, when you're left with the airy

froth of memory, the sweet cold of it on your tongue,
the cold sweat of the blue glass in your hand.

NEWCOMER

She's 9, black-haired, with her mother
just off the train from Norfolk to San Diego.
It's mid-year at US Grant Elementary
where she's now enrolled. Before,

she lived in Bremerton, near the Naval
Shipyard. Roosevelt is the new president.
No one has heard of Pearl Harbor,
five years away from infamy.

She wears the plaid skirt her mother made
and has on her black and white Oxfords,
polished that very morning.
She stands before the class, introduced

by the young teacher, Miss Cohon,
who says Please make our new friend
feel at home. She has traveled a long way,
almost 3000 miles, to be with us today.

The girl can't bring herself to lift her eyes
to see the 30 odd faces boring into her
from their wooden desks. Miss Cohon bends
to the girl staring at the gray linoleum,

You know, we have something in common.
I'm new too. My home is far away,
in a city called Huntsville. You and I,
we're both newcomers together.

In telling her story, the girl—now 93,
feet slippered, knees quilt-covered
where she sits on the cat-clawed sofa—
pauses, her voice catching. On the wall

behind are her sumi-e paintings: a catfish,
a curled cat, a chrysanthemum. Two minutes
pass before she can go on. That fall,
she says, we came home at last to Bremerton.

SHELL

Waves and rocks have nicked the outer edge.
Ugly shell. No one, not even me, would
bend on this wind-slapped shore to pry it out
of sand. Uses: soap dish, small ashtray, cup,
scoop, spoon, scraper, knife. Or a boat to the moon
for a Haida girl, born, I'll guess, near Juneau,
circa 1830. I picture her digging clams
on the beaches of Douglas Island
where she lived with her Wolf Clan.

That would be before the Jesuits
took her Indian name, baptized her
as *Catherine,* solemnized her marriage
to a Québécois trader in the employ
of the Hudson's Bay Company. Loving
certain unpretty things, as I do,
beautifully ugly things, she'd have loved
my shell, admired it, played with it
a while, then flung it into the waves.

The interior glistens as if lacquered
with moonlight—a pearly nacre the clam
extrudes to adorn its hinged apartment.
Outwardly, it's a homely dwelling.
Holding it up to the evening sun,
enough light—just enough—enters through
the calcium carbonate layers,
through the lustrous inner cowl—to reveal
a mountain range at twilight, haloed

by a thin line of clouds, all seen as if
from across an expanse of water.
Inside the shell, the sun illumines
a wonder of bright imperfections:
specks of sand, they may well be, or flakes
of mica, suspended in the matrix, aglow
when I turn the shell, some appearing as stars
above the mountains, some below as the fires
of a village from a vanished age.

IMMIGRANTS

I've spent entire days lost in the warehouses
of dust, searching the archives, imagining my ancestors
boarding ships for America, leaving the coal mines
of Cornwall, only to end in Wright County, Iowa,
in an untended graveyard wedged between a corn field
and the Union Pacific line, their stones toppled,
their names scrubbed by a hundred fifty winters
to an indecipherable blur.

I leave them in their moldering beds to stroll the garden,
drawn by a rufous hummingbird needling the feeder,
his head a burst of copper in the angled morning light.
I love how he bobs among the squash blossoms,
barging into one yellow mansion, then another,
insatiable, as I am, at times, impatient to say
the unsayable, wondering what difference it makes
to the finches bickering in the laurel hedge.

I go out again at dusk. He's still there, levitating
among the blossoming beans, seeking a droplet
from each white beaker. Then he's gone,
leaving me with my ancestors and their beards,
bonnets and gold timepieces. Farms failed.
Over in Illinois, the Savoys upped stakes,
arriving by train at Puget Sound, dumbstruck by the girth
of doug firs and hemlocks bejeweled by April rain.

William, Josie and the new baby, Birdy, trundled toward
a logging camp near Bremerton, bouncing in a wagon
to the end of a mud-gummed road. Might they not have
passed thickets of wild rose? Might they not have seen
those same flashes of copper, startled by the furious
whir of hundreds of rufous hummers, themselves
migrants from Mexico? I want to think so.
I want to think Josie, exhausted from the journey,
said to her baby, That's honeysuckle, sweetheart,
as their buckboard came within hearing
of the rasp of whipsaws, the scream of a steam whistle,
and the crash of a felled cedar in this, their new home.

VIEW OF RICHMOND BEACH

What I love is the rasp of small waves,
the sound of the Sound, that slap of flat green glass,
and to scale the bluff and read the names on graves—
Lund, Weiss, Baby Matsue, lost in uncut grass.

A cloud turns rosy like Anders' plastic flower.
Sister, lover, father—flowers meant to nullify decay.
Comes a time our ordinary star will lose its power,
the lighthouse light will flicker, life will sail away.

There's a cheery thought. The bluff sheers off at my feet.
My sons once ran on that sand, threw shells
and skippers. Crows tumble like tatters of a burnt sheet
to roost down-beach where they cast their spells.

Dark comes on. Far out, a ferry glitters its way
to Vashon Island, bearing the last light of day.

ASH

That small word came to you by some odd
synaptic path. A meteoroid skipped off
your atmosphere, some bit of stellar shrapnel
from so far away "far away" means nothing.

It might have been the thread of fire
just over the ridge, caught in the corner
of your jaded eye, extinguished
by the time you grabbed its tail.

That led to other kinds of flare-ups:
a conflagration of roses out back,
bursting overnight, gaudy and heartbreaking
for reasons reasonable to you alone:

you were there. By Wednesday
they had fallen, one brown petal after another,
like burnt potato chips on the lawn.
Like ash. Then there was the heat you felt

at thirteen, lying on the dock,
nettles of lake water singeing your back.
You still see, under your splayed elbow,
through wet lashes, a prismatic world.

You still see the down on her arm, small
swellings through her thin green suit
pressed against the boards.
That's when, as night fell, you understood

the ache of life. She grabbed your wrist. *Wow,*
she said. *Shooting star!* You missed it. Years travel
quicker than tonight's grain of iron sparking
off the ridge. Her name—Meredith—leaps back

with the plash of ducks paddling in the dark.
She's that half-second flash of fire returned
from space deep in your aging brain, rendered,
as she has surely ended, as you will end, as ash.

COFFEE

We hike with mugs to a nearby creek,
there to smell and drink the light, pass the time
we have left together, one last hill to climb
that will show us where we've been. We speak
or, rather, joke about who'll go first, is the soul
a cloud, or what about that morning a brown bear
caught us in the act? You're the more aware,
the one who sees the rapids ahead, the goal
not to get there but to go there. Love, you
were always better at fending off the pressure
of regret, disillusionment. You see pleasure
in morning rain. How would I go on? How do
I—or you—stand alone in willow shade, a place
where we kissed, no longer face to face?

Four: Presence

Crows do not reserve their vocal discourse for one another; sometimes they talk directly to us.

~Lyanda Lynn Haupt, from her book *Crow Planet, p. 79*

THE PATH

Last night's rain brought down
needles from the big pine,
quilting the path to the river

whose heavy breathing is not so much
like music — more like wind
rasping in the aspens.

Leaves glitter with river color—
the air sweet from pine pitch.
Patches of hillside orange

flare and smear on the current
blended with blue afternoon.
A heron glides upstream

toward the deeper tones of evening.
On the far shore, in a hemlock snag,
a pair of cedar waxwings loop

back and forth to feed on mayflies,
whose wings are flakes of light
rising and falling over the river.

POETRY CLASS

I wish I'd liked her more. She'd stand heron-still in the hall,
her Goth-black hair damp, inky, lank on her spindly shoulders.

She'd greet me with a pursed smile, erase it and hold open the door.
In the early weeks she'd sprawl in her back row chair, yawn,

check her phone, text a friend, watch—or appear to watch—
sparrows dart about in the camellia tree out the classroom window.

Now and then she'd fish for something in her bag.
A string of badly tattooed stars wandered up her forearm.

Two lip rings and eye shadow failed to highlight the natural wonder
of her kelp-green eyes. She rarely spoke. Her soft flat voice

muffled some anger, some sadness she had packed away
in her private attic. Her poems of exploding roses or crows

without beaks were edgy, hard to follow, as if she could care less
if people understood. Still, she'd come to class with copies,

read them in her almost audible monotone, then face the predictable
bewildered silence, broken when one of her two allies

said, "Whoa! Cool!" Or when a non-ally piped up: "Uh, I'm lost."
I'd add something like, "Well, it's rough but, as always, it depends

where you go from here. I see promise." To my surprise,
she'd revise, even when not requested. And the poems got crisper,

stranger, more obliquely and less directly personal, sometimes
blackly funny, as when she likened a boy she once dated

to Gandhi in one stanza, Al Capone in the next. She'd vanish
for two weeks, then appear again with a new piercing and,

I was startled to see, a bright smile, as if some good thing
had lifted her to a new level of confidence or consciousness,

accompanied by what I saw as a breakthrough in her poems,
in particular one about bats asleep by day in their cave,

protected, keeping each other warm, mother bats nursing their young,
and then, at twilight, so she wrote, "they gush into the sky

like an alphabet." I didn't comment when she read it to the class
but looked her way at the end of the conference table,

clicked my tongue and clenched my fist—my silent way
of saying *Yes! This one sings!* At the end of the period,

 I said, "Genevieve, the term's almost over. We need to talk
about your missed assignments." "I know," she said,

"but not today. I gotta take my boyfriend to the clinic."
Her boyfriend stabbed her to death that weekend

in an apartment across town. I didn't learn this news
till the start of the new term. Alone in my office, I read

copies of her earlier work. Those about her boyfriend
now became tragic, prescient with hints. Later poems showed

a young person diving into language, in love with consonants:
Bs, Vs, the hard C of cave, the fire of the letter R.

I've visited her grave. I did not speak to Genevieve as if
she was a secret lover and could hear my pained confession.

Roethke did that in "Elegy for Jane." Still, I've kept a folder
of her work, including one with my margin scribbles,

suggesting where she might open the poem's door to let in more
of her particular light and dark. She never saw my half-legible jottings,

likely written just days after her death. There she stands again,
in the hall, rucksack slung on her shoulder, holding the door for me.

Welcome back, Genevieve. Happy to be here, she says, her eyes vivid.
Again I see how tall she is, how rail-thin, find I'm still unconvinced

by the black mascara and dyed hair, startled, almost breathless by her
green gaze, her irises I'd never noticed—till now—flecked with gold.

THE LESSON

Red-eyed, mascara smeared, she slumps in her chair
against the back wall. Above her, the clock glowers,
fast one day, slow the next, begrudging its hours.
Scarlet highlights inflame her graying hair.

She fishes a tissue from her tattered purse.
I've recited a poem about a son
saying goodbye to his father. I alone
see her daub her cheeks from the edge of the class.

The others half-listen, their young, bored
faces unreadable. From her cloister,
she mouths the words "So sorry." Her lips quiver.
She knows too well what the others haven't heard—

a poem can unlock grief and set it free.
Now it's her I read. She knows the son is me.

SPOON

Thrift store find. Fifty cents. I like how stout
it is, carved of some uncertain hardwood,
one black scar on the handle suggesting
its owner snatched it off a hot burner.

I like the wear on the tip of the spoon.
Someone stirred and stirred, sanding the right side
of the bowl to near-flatness—the stirrer
left-handed, it appears, more than likely

a woman, perhaps living—wild surmise—
in Iowa in the thirties, baby
balanced on her right hip while she stands
in the heat of her Monarch cast iron stove

stirring porridge or corn mush or mutton stew.
Now it's my turn to keep milk from scalding,
milk into which I will stir chocolate
pudding powder. It's three a.m., the third

of January. I can't claim to see
the light snow that dusts the cars parked out front,
since I'm at the stove stirring the pudding.
I can, however, see grains fall like salt

on the outer sill of the near kitchen window,
just as she too might have seen snow
or rain fall as she stood and stirred, switching
hands when her left grew tired, as my left hand

does now. Yes, it was a woman who carved
the much-used spoon in my hand. And if not
on an Iowa farm, then somewhere else,
preparing countless meals, hanging the spoon

on its nail, through the augured off-center
hole in the handle, taking down the spoon,
putting it on its nail, taking it down,
putting it on, down, on, the years passing,

kids having grown and left the farm, removed,
I'd venture, to the city. So the spoon
contains all the sadness of her left hand.
Even the spoon journeyed away from her,

settling against all odds in my kitchen
to stir the just-now-bubbling pudding.
It's as if I've entered another life,
one where I cook, clean, give birth, raise children,

watch snow whiten a stack of cordwood.
It's as if she's beside me as I write, as if she has
given me the spoon and taken my free hand
in hers to stroll the garden of our two worlds.

DEAR FRIEND

I was not a good friend, and that's a gun to the heart,
a fist to the soul's gut. Gut. Where your cancer struck,
boom! One night you were alone in a hotel in…where was it?
Maybe Bogotá. I'm at loose end as always, every time
I want to speak or write to you. So. Hotel in Bogotá,

we'll say, where one night the gut pain came as a full moon
on the dirty window, moon of dull ache, not moon
of food poisoning, which in your travels you no doubt encountered
in fair measure. I'm not a good friend, still, dear friend.
I never wrote after your daughter's birth, your life

in Boston, the appearance—and disappearance—
of your only published novel, your sundry jobs—
textbook rep, bus driver, drugstore clerk. Steve,
I'm writing now. Please don't call it pointless, though it is.
Please permit me to remember that simmering day in July,

me just off the train, drugged by sleeplessness
from the all-night jerk and clank, Seattle to Missoula,
my new next home, lugging backpack and suitcase
across the Clark Fork Bridge. There you sat
on the porch of your run-down rental. Straw-hatted

you were, shirtless, beer bottle balanced on the arm of a rocker.
I stopped to ask directions—first person I'd talked to in a day,
first Montanan I talked to ever. That was then, dear friend.
Years are dew on grass, gone by noon. Bad friend, call me,
for my neglect, for the way time knifes the cord that bound us

for a time. I tracked your daughter down only to learn
you died twelve years ago from the cancer that chewed away
till the moon, dear friend, no longer shone in any window anywhere.
What becomes of those we once loved once the train door closes,
one of us aboard, the other waving, exiting the station

with no umbrella against the rain, nothing to do but walk
the city street all night? I write to say so long, dear friend,
aware of the absurdity of saying it this way, twelve years late.
In ways I won't even try to explain, crossing
the Clark Fork Bridge, spying you on the porch,

I knew I'd outlive you. I knew you'd leave Helen for another woman.
I knew your daughter would care for you in your last days.
I knew I'd locate her in Fresno, not one week ago.
I even knew, after Montana, I'd lose track, that I'd one day
look back to realize, after Montana, I'd never see you again.

LETTER TO J, TWO DAYS AFTER HER DEATH

-Montagnac, France

A friend calls your poems "perfectly cut gemstones."
I couldn't have said, having never read your work—
until last night. Yes. Gemstones. Light-filled.
Will they endure? Doubtful. It doesn't matter now.
The sun has gone down on the first day of eternity,
that winding cavern whose walls are adorned
with animals no one can remember
having roamed here. Yesterday, this place was ice,
then tundra, now a town with a cell tower taller
than the bell tower of its 14th century church.

In my best bad French, I've ordered *café au lait*
and a croissant. Across the lane from this *patisserie,*
the church's ancient door glares, barricaded,
a weathered poster announcing what I gather says
"Closed for Repairs." The dour saints carved
in the door's cracked oak could be mistaken
for those two old men at the table to my left
smoking *Gauloises,* nursing their tiny coffees,
frowning at today's *Le Monde*, their eyes
more doleful than the sainted faces across the way.

As if you care, in light of where you are—
I stayed up half the night, opened to you,
my damp hotel room cramped as a cave shelf,
water-worn by the eons, the drip of time.
I set your life aside and saw again

bison, ibex, a black-maned yellow horse,
reindeer fording a swollen stone river,
only their antlered heads above water—
all painted by flicker of oil lamp—
all alive and moving on the walls

of nearby Lascaux cave. Good tourist,
I spend three hours gawking with the herd
in the cave's chilled remote interiors.
Some of the animals turn their heads to observe
the observers, our dim faces rivering
though the hollowed vaults and chambers.
Calcite walls suddenly become 3-D.
Seams and bulges appear to flow
along natural contours of the rock,
transformed by art into backs, bellies and hooves.

Even the high ceilings are painted,
as if the cosmos was itself a bestiary,
the sky a great pasture grazed by the creatures
of our dreams. No trees in this region back then,
no wood with which to make scaffold.
And you, friend? What mysterious scaffold
did you build to access your most private niches?
Reading your book, I think I know: words were ladders
to climb and descend. One thin ladder-like poem
recounts your daughter's suicide, how,

fighting traffic and tears, you drove miles
to find a Salvation-Army drop-box.
You deposited a bag of her clothes,

neatly folded, saving only several
of her *Nirvana* CDs, a poster signed
by Kurt Cobain, who, you say in the poem,
called to her from a darkened concert hall.
No trace of self-pity in your quiet elegy.
That's why I find it crushing, unbearable,
the spare rungs of its lines so lean, so luminous,

it's as if you've borne a daughter's death
to some higher point of clarity—
a mountain lookout of contemplative grief.
In another poem, you walk a lakeshore
at dawn, startling—being startled by—
a great blue heron lifting off a limb
just above your head. You speak of being stunned
by the heron's deep-throated squawk of alarm—
a *sob* you call it in the poem. You describe
the shudder of wings in your chest,

the shattered air, the rain of nesting twigs
showering you as you stood on the path
among cattails trying to make sense
of the sense of being in the presence
of some majestic being skimming inches
over the lake's morning mirror.
In the poem, you follow the heron's legs
trailing the blue of its great body to where
it settles on a stump on the farther shore,
alighting delicately as a tremor on the lake.
The cry was your own, the poem reveals,
the sob you made at the birth of your only child.

An obelisk stands in grass outside the church.
Its four sides list the village boys who died
in the Great War, their names grouped alphabetically,
brothers and cousins together, incised in marble
blackened by a century of sun, rain,
car exhaust. Long list for a small town.
Nos chers enfants, says the plaque, its words
implacable as the gaze of the carved saints.

J, you died from wounds in that other Great War,
that nobler campaign to paint or carve or write
the heart's winding chronicle, to discover
the cave of beautiful beings, to see them
move their ponderous haunches, hear them
snort and low, chuffing as they shift on the walls.
The artists took their tools and lamps, sealed
the entry 200 centuries ago and, with no illusions,
walked away to wait for us to find their gallery.
J, I agree: It's preposterous for me to believe

the dead remember what it's like to breathe.
That admitted, I want you to know your book
lay beside me last night in the bad bed
in Montignac. I've discovered the entry.
I've read what you incised, seen the creatures
you made by blowing paint through reeds
to animate inanimate stone. J, you need not wait
for 20,000 years. I've lifted my lamp.
I've glimpsed your deep interiors,
the moving images you left behind.

PINE SISKIN

Small thing, the black seeds
of your eyes will never see day again,
never again cloud or weed.

The window killed you—
the clarity of it, appearing as air,
your branch mirrored in its false tree.

I heard the thump and knew
you wouldn't live—too loud
not to be fatal on this first bright

April afternoon. A jay guffaws. Robins
call for mates, or warn outsiders
to stay outside the glass of understanding,

glass that divides in from out,
my world from theirs, yours.
In a few minutes, the sun will fail,

still aflame in the tops of firs
along the drive. Plum-like,
you weigh little more than a dime

in my palm. The speck of blood
on your head means nothing now.
Your yellow wing bars, nothing.

Nor your ivory rice-grain beak,
nor your twiggy feet, drawn inward.
I'll trowel you a grave, friend,

in the ground where this morning
I planted peas. The first rhododendrons
are primed to burst into wads

of gaudy fire. Wondrous is the last light.
Wondrous, a cloud of crows
languid in the evening sky.

Wondrous, the hum of the earth,
reddish glow in trees. Wondrous, too,
when the fire flickers, falters and dies.

CHICKADEES AT THE FEEDER

Light and looping they drop in from across
the street, a neighbor's lawn or shrub, to dally
in the bare lilac tree near our feeder.
I'm their seed man. They draw my attention
with their black toupees and buzzy chatter.
It doesn't matter a whit who feeds them.
They come for what's available, as,
I suppose, I do myself, though I've yet to learn
how to make those insistent bits of sound,
how to give the world flashes of chestnut and bone
white as they do, perched on the phone line.
In this life, you take what you can get and
if there's time enough give back some small thing,
some wedge of joy, even if you fiction it.
For now, for this given day, I'm happy
to fill the feeder once again. Later,
they'll scoot off to the next yard where shadows
deepen. No guarantees of food or water.
That's the way it is in this life and, most likely,
the other. There is no "other," of course.
Just this one. Your job, you gadabouts,
is to keep an eye on the gray cat below
the rose, who has all the time in the world
to wait for your false move, your two-second
lapse of attention when a black spot of earth
shows promise, you go there, and it's over.
Not over today, however. The rhodies
are the colors of real and unreal fire,

smoldering for a single brilliant week.
That's the way it is in this life—the brief one—
and the other as well, creased and folded inside
the first. It's the second life that dazzles forever.

NEW YEAR'S EVE

Two years now since your young heart stopped.
I never had what it takes to start it or stop
the father in my head saying *Hearts go wrong,*
they stop even when there's nothing wrong,
even as the sun rises inside my chest, rises
routinely from the sea, from mountains, rises,
rises and then one day it does not rise.
Two years. New Year's Eve, my dear young one.
The EMTs shocked you back, threw not one
but three electric punches. *He's gone,* they said. *Gone.*
I never had what it takes to bear that word, "gone,"
that fatal punch to the heart, so final,
gone from the gold world. Your heart woke, finally,
to gift a second, a third, a fourth chance.
It wasn't luck or God. Still, one chance
in a million, New Years Eve, red lights
aflame in the trees, fire trucks, cruisers, lights
awhirl like blue acetylene, you, gray-faced,
gurneyed into the aid car, revived, your face
intubated, slack by the induced coma, but revived,
the aid car shrieking away. *Revived! Revived!*
Dear young one, I have what it takes
to step from grief to muted joy, to take
what is dispensed by the random hand
extended from the ether, to hold you and
feel your living fingers in my hand.

PRESENCE

There's the ridge again through leafless limbs.
A heron follows the river upstream,
deep into the blue. In the sharp winter light,
aspen shadows crisscross the snow—
a foreshadowing of their falling: flood, age,
disease, a beaver's incisive jaws.

Walker's pasture sundials the afternoon.
Long shadows glide blade-like
across the snow, sheering tufts of tan grass
in a cutting too slow for the eye,
too quick for the mind. Shadows vanish.
The blue deepens. A scatter of leaves

skitters like paper coins—a coinage no one
will possess. A solitary thrush feeds on the last
frozen chokecherries. No sound other than
the river hushing, muted by a line of cottonwoods.
No moon. No stars, though the first several
will soon appear above the peak of Walker's barn.

In the time it takes me to wade the drifts,
lift, duck under and replace a loose fence rail,
slog my way in the dark to a looming form,
a thousand stars will have awakened, sending
just enough light to print on the snow
the spidery lacework of an apple tree.

FACEBOOK

Thanks, my peeps, for your concern. I'm still in shock.
Just now watered the tomatoes. BTW,
Paris was *magnifique* this spring. A walk
along the Seine can really make your day.
It made mine, *en tout cas*. And Musée d'Orsay!
Wow! You gotta see *L'Origin du Monde*.
That was then, this is now. Good to be back,
though it's lonely here. Has anyone owned
a Smart Car? Shit. Disc is full on my Mac.
Ideas? Tech support has a worthless FAQ.
Doing my best to deal with emptiness.
At least there's you. And there's Funny or Die.
And my irises, my purple tongues of sadness.
They sing today. Without them, I'd want to cry.

NEIGHBORHOOD CROWS

In lazy flight this afternoon, they resemble
scraps of crepe blown aloft above the sunlit
crowns of firs. They're my aloof neighbors.
All their guttural utterances are black, cynical,

feathered with irony. *The point is,* they mutter,
there's no point. They clean up our messes.
In the corner of a field they hop to a scrap
of burger still in its silver wrapper.

Tolerant as Lao Tzu, plain as nickels, they gather
on wires in squads of nine. Earning a living,
they know, depends on luck, a canny eye
and magic, which explains their sorcerer's robes,

glossy as lacquered shadows at twilight.
Like the universe, they do not judge.
They have no comment on the divorce rate
or the attendance of gangsters at church.

Instead, they're the lamplighters of old, lighting stars
to signal day's end as they pass over power lines.
Imponderable, ordinary, like night itself,
they spread their wings to shelter their young,

invite their friends to dinner in a ditch
or near an upturned garbage can. When threatened
by a hawk they call in reinforcements to harry
the intruder, distracting hunter away from the hunted.

At dawn they reappear, routine as soot
but wiser. For crows are learned monks
in vacant lots, beggars who take the vow
of poverty and then take over the city.

Crows have nothing to teach, nothing to sell.
They joke, cajole, bicker and tend
to their families. They are Zen masters
of the art of blending in, always making the best

of a bad situation, as poets do who know
it's hopeless but go on anyway with their crow visions
and dark pronouncements, feigning nonchalance
when we fail to understand their off-the-cuff

commentaries, those suggestions they offer in order
to survive the coming apocalypse. If we paid attention,
we might even learn something—not merely
how to face the day when the comet strikes or the missiles

rise from their silos, but how to live in the now,
how to start anew, how to be better than we've been
and, despite the madness of our time,
how to get along with our neighbors, how to thrive.

WASHING OUR BACKS

We'd stand under the shower in that shabby rental
we made livable, somehow, despite the broken water heater.
Scalding needles or ice pellets—you never knew
what might rain down from the dangling fixture,

crusted with Depression-era rust. You preferred
a coarse cloth, usually blue. I liked threadbare,
soap-scum gray. We'd press together, breast-to-breast,
right arms clapped around the other's back to scrub,

you requesting firm. *Give it elbow grease,* you'd say.
I favored long light strokes. We'd embrace as if to fuse
into one person, our eel-slick skin sex-enlivened,
aware of itself, touched as if for the first time, braced

for that moment we might cry out from a gush, ice or fire.
We'd slow-dance without moving much in the space allotted,
the tub floor slippery as butter. All we could hold onto
was each other. It's a miracle we never fell. Once, you gripped

my wrists hard enough to leave welts. Next day, a student
came up before class. *Brawling again, I see,* she smiled.
And we brawl still, in the shower, more gently now.
We still wash each other into lathers of pleasure,

shoulder blades first—those incipient wings
that keep us grounded—then down the spine, back up,
hips to ribs to underarms, me giving it elbow grease
with your coarse cloth, you swabbing me

with my tattered filament. All the while our free hands
roam freely through the countryside of our bodies,
remembering favorite routes, those hills and dales
our hands love to find. And then, oh, then, we kiss.

Five: Airborne

And so a couple
Of years ago,
The old poets died
Young.

And now the young,
Scarlet on their wings, fly away
Over the marshes.

~James Wright, from "An Elegy for the Poet Morgan Blum," from *Above the River: The Complete Poems of James Wright*

SWING

It's that sensation of plunge and rise,
of growing heavy and light and heavy
and light, of forward-leaning and backward-leaning,
legs tucked, legs thrust out,
the one-second release from gravity,
toes pointed at clouds, neck craned,
head groundward back-tipped,
hair swept to and fro, brushing the dust,
the iron links cold and shrill,
silent at the arc ends, unburdened
for the periodic instances, then whining
with your weight for a full hour,
the tool shed falling as you rise,
rising as you fall, then from the head-low-
legs-high view, the derelict green house
inverted, half its windows broken—
a Titanic made of ice—that sensation,
the peaks and valleys of dizziness
flooding you, draining from you
with each pump and lunge until
that moment when, having pulled
and pulled to lift yourself beyond
yourself, straining, almost parallel
to the wincing crossbeam, you shift your grip
on the chains, readying for launch
at maximum forward upward speed,
whereupon you jettison into the dusk
of your ninth September, lofted into a brief

parabola over a coil of green garden hose,
a wheelbarrow full of rainwater,
and an upturned rake, its teeth bared,
entirely ready to puncture your life—
and with arms flailing, once in every five
or six leaps, you land feet first into the cool
end of summer. The jolt when you hit
the ground, upright in victory or sprawled
on the beaten grass, inhaling its green musk,
feeling grit and sweat on your neck—
that sensation is why you adjust the rake
a little farther out, edged closer
to the furrow your impacts have dug,
to see precisely how far you can fly, to learn
by how much or how little you're able
to clear that row of rust red teeth.

MEADOWLARK

He's out there, somewhere, a quarter mile off,
hidden in the crown of that lightning-struck pine.
At this distance, maybe he's not there, maybe his voice
is there, careening across Rocky Flats, indigoed
with camas and larkspur—wild with shooting star.

His phrases carry from his pine to here,
the ground patched with monk's hood, cowled
like its name, among lichen-ladened scree.
She I love prowls the near-treeless meadow,
pausing to listen, binoculars aimed,

scanning for bluebirds in the wind-combed grass.
That's when the long, twisted, complicated notes
come tumbling in a trick of acoustics to fill the expanse.
The pine hunches, blasted one night a hundred years ago,
arthritic now, a misshapen thing persevering

alone with the flowers, stones, wind, droppings
of deer and elk who have heard the same arias
sail out from deep within the green. I tell myself
it's music. It is not music, not in the mind
of a meadowlark. Still, it's a wondrous sound

nevertheless, a little delirious, the complex notes
alarming in their urgency: *I'm alive, you fools!*
All that matters are the sun-fringed clouds.
Wake up! All that matters are the sun-fringed clouds.
She I love scans the lightning-struck pine.

Who's his audience? There it is: the mystery
of poetry. Other meadowlarks, of course. Of course
the stones, the flowers, droppings of deer and elk.
Maybe the lightning-struck pine he's in, maybe
she I love, blue-parka-ed, her ears cupped to hear.

BAT IN DAYLIGHT

So balletic are his leaps and swoops,
his gray-brown 4-inch wings so agile
he seems an angel, a leaf
fallen from an aspen, slightly daft
as if attached to clear fishing line
tied to a girl's finger. He traces
filigrees above the pump house,
near my heap of pine rounds
split for winter. Why he's here
in early September I have no idea—
a nocturnal insomniac, I gather,
like me, out hunting, drawn perhaps
by the scent of pine pitch or, more likely,
flying ants I've seen rising from beneath
a stump. Easy prey. Such deft moves.
An ant's wings flutter down like tiny
transparent oars, lighting on a round
my ax is buried in. Off he veers.
The mystery of his appearance remains,
like the mystery of night and day,
or bat aerobatics, or the human roundness
of the hill across the river,
river shimmer, river clatter, muted now in fall,
chitter of a kingfisher cruising
upstream and down. Or the mystery
of dusk, when bats usually waken,
peel off from spaces in the roof shakes,
then zigzag above the cottonwoods,

writing calligraphy in the deepening blue,
writing their lives all night—
but for the one who may emerge at dawn
while others return to their shake beds,
squeaking and scratching.
He's the oddball, the contrarian,
the one who works the day shift,
who must do things his way, even if
it means he's out alone, curious to see
(though half-blind) river glitter
or what trees look like, the daytime moon
or wonder if he should be afraid
of the large creature below,
grunting and sweating, affixed
to the earth, staring up at him.

THE UNFOCUSED EYES OF DRONES

They're dream wrens in the clear lake of day,
like toys, a slightly larger replica
of those model planes men play with
at the park on weekends to escape the house.

One of them, Chuck, lives near me.
I see him summer afternoons, alone
on the baseball diamond's pitcher's mound.
He flies a delicate Sopwith Camel biplane,

then a screaming Spitfire that frightens a park dog.
He barrel-rolls his planes, gliding on some
unnamed emotion wired to his remote control.
You could say Chuck, the operator,

is well-rounded in his "Beer Beats Sex" tee shirt.
He's got Santa's beard and Trotsky's glasses.
He wouldn't harm a soul, though he lives
in a country that harms souls every day.

He may well know drones have been taught to think,
to beam down and detect human auras.
When its blue brain glows red, darts fly out,
quieter than starlight aimed at desert flowers.

The operator sits in a quiet room
playing the controls somewhere deep inside
the American Heartland—Ohio,
say, or Nebraska. He does not ask

who the girl in the red headscarf might be,
seen moving across his monitor
in what appears to be a courtyard filled
with trees, most likely lemon. She waters

a bed of eggplants with a plastic bottle
that could in his mind be a bomb
she plans to plant by the nearby roadside.
Crickets fill the air with their raspy chorus.

The operator can't hear them, nor does he
know her scarf is red. He sees only
the flash of light on his screen, sees
an opened rose made of pieces of the girl's house:

brick, rock, glass, iron, paper, threads
from her headscarf, seen on the screen
in various tones of gray and sepia,
a roiling miasma seeping outward

from the courtyard. When the last
chunk of mortar has fallen, the last
of the seared leaves flutters down,
the mist of lemons hovers in the air.

WHITMAN READING BY MOONLIGHT

Walt Whitman pads around on the lawn
in bathrobe and slippers. Moonlight
silvers the lilac tree by the dooryard,
the flowers long gone from lavender to rust.
He opens his notebook to read a recent draft,
the title appearing as—he can't make it out—
"Growing Broken Berry," it looks like.
Back in bed he sees himself forlorn,
alone on the stern, riding the Brooklyn Ferry,
his shirt collar turned up, his fingers
clutching the brim of his straw hat.
He opens his notebook and reads aloud
by moonlight a draft, its working title:
"Crossing Brooklyn Ferry." In bed,
staring at the black screen of the ceiling,
he watches himself tear out one page
from the notebook, then another.
When he releases them, they rise like gulls
aloft on the back draft, awhirl in a billow
of coal smoke and steam. Pages flutter
ungainly, as if wounded, alighting
on the wake's white fire where they swim,
swirl, flatten and disappear
into the black waters of the Hudson.

AIRBORNE

What comes back are two seconds
of weightlessness. That and a dirt road,
purple foxglove in a ditch,
the crunch of gravel under the red
tractor's great black wheels.
There's the grind and smoke
of a belabored engine downshifted
against the steep down-grade
toward a cave of cedars erasing
all but quilt scraps of sunlight.
There's me propped on his lap,
full of the smell of him—Old Spice,
pipe tobacco breast-pocketed
in his overalls, pipe and pouch
pressed against my back, his fat hands
on the steering wheel, my small hands
tight on it, alive with vibration
this fall morning now startled
by the gunfire of backfire, startled
again by silence, again by lurch,
release, by sudden speed, his quiet "Hold on,"
our trailer of firewood careening,
whipped side to side, chunks lofted,
his foot stomped on the useless brake.
There are the two beautiful seconds
where I'm lifted free from the weight
of my childhood, of the fables I'd made,
lifted, flung from the jackknifed

tractor about to roll, struck in the back
by some hard thing, he leaping after me,
my face pushed in the muck of the ditch
where I flop entirely awake
to the tops of trees, bits of blue,
aware that there's no end to it,
there's an end to it. I'm not able
to breathe or cry or feel
thorns of blackberry in my cheek,
the sting of nettles in this,
the new life, the one in which
nothing is sure, everything governed
by the immutable Law of the Unforeseen.
I hear the hoarse rasp of my name,
see his bloodied head near mine
when he lifts me from the brambles.
I'm able then to taste the ditch,
spit muck and bits of leaves,
able now to understand he threw me
to save me, able still to see myself
in his arms as he carried me up the hill,
aware of being aware of the light perfume
of wild roses crushed where I'd landed,
petals matted in my muddied hair.

GIRLS JUMPING ROPE

Three girls, brown-skinned and pigtailed—sisters,
from the look of their high cheekbones, their wide
bright eyes—have tied two lengths of clothesline

to the fender of a parked car. The tallest swings each line
in a dizzy clockwise-counterclockwise braid.

The ropes whir as they gyre the air.
Into these humming ovals the younger sisters leap,
their skip-hopping feet hardly touching the asphalt,

as if it might be lava. How hot it is! The soft tap
of their sneakers syncopates with the snap of the ropes.

So lithe are they, so graceful, so synchronous
in their timing, their fine-tuned turning, you want to weep
at the beauty of the human form in motion.

After ten minutes a rope catches an ankle,
the jumping stops, and the three girls, who have not

uttered a sound till then, burst into the laughter
of girlhood, a pure shrieking deep-down joy,
their thin chests heaving, sweat-sheen on their brows

and bare arms. You applaud. For the first time,
they notice you on the curb and bow grandly.

The youngest girl—she might be 10—becomes the twirler.
They could not care less what's in your head, your attic
of dark thoughts, or your heart, heavy as a rucksack

of anvils. Never mind all that. Your sparrows of despair
lift into the sultry August evening as much for the artistry

of the skipping girls as for the music of their soul-igniting
laughter. About those plans you had to head for the hills,
far from the thrones of power, to join the ghosts

of Cistercians in the ruins of Tintern Abbey, renouncing
all but the earth, to live as an ascetic pure as the currents

of the River Wye, to leave behind the Forbidden City
and its emperor, Cronus, he who eats his children
once they have voted for him, to retreat forever

on the gauzy side of a Chinese screen of mountain mist—
those plans are now on hold. You've decided to honor

your contract with the living world, to sit on this curb
and watch them, the Three Graces, jump once more.
The sun drops behind a garish billboard enticing the young

to join the Marines. A street light blinks on, its radiant cone
spotlighting the girls, their bodies a blur inside the whir

of the clotheslines. From their bleachers in heaven, the gods—
Dionysus and Aphrodite most noticeably—clap, stomp
their feet and cheer like the justly proud parents they are.

Six: Union Creek in Winter

....I see her mother's face, beaten and
beaten into the shape of a plant,
a cactus with grey spines and broad
dark maroon blooms.
I see her arm stretched out across her baby,
wrist resting, heavily, still across the
tiny ribs.
                    Don't speak to me about
politics. I've got eyes, man.

~From Sharon Olds' poem "The Issues," from her book *The Dead and the Living*

UNION CREEK IN WINTER

There's no word for it so far, the word
for what it means to be in love with you
in our sinking world, what it means to hike
through new snow, to hear beneath
the glass of creek ice the flow of winter
percolating its way through the ravine
not quite soundlessly toward lower ground
to join the wild roar of the American River.

The word that means we've loved
through the avalanches of our time,
loved while the wars raged, paid for
with our taxes, loved while our loved ones
voted for hatred, for *I-want-the-false-past-I-want-
what's-coming-to-me,* protected as they've been
by their skin white as this very snow draped
on hemlocks in the ravine's wavering light.

The word that means we're not alone,
we share that same nature wonder,
for the flicker tapping on a far-off tree,
the delicate calligraphy of a mouse's
prints along our path, as if Tu Fu
has been here too, who knew, even then,
even in the Tang Dynasty, beauty
leaves behind its faint notations.

The word that means we will go on,
we will follow an earlier trekker's snowshoe
trail, slog on bundled to keep the chill
from overtaking us, descend again steeply,
then climb again switchbacks above the creek
away from its cold murmurings, to our car
and the long drive back to the war zone
of now. Armed with our little courage,

we must drive straight to the front,
strap on flak jackets and begin the slow
search for survivors, slow search
for the words that might revive them.
Even now we're feverish to make contact,
to know what to listen for, to learn to hear
those muffled cries from deep in the rubble.
If we knew the words we might save

those most weakened, most in danger of giving up.
If we knew the words we might keep the world,
its rivers, its ice, its bitterroot, its winter wrens,
its hemlocks, its moonlight, its children,
its Shakespeare, its Szymborska, its rosehips,
its green and orange lichens, its Dylan,
its kora players, its hummingbirds, you,
me, and our Muslim neighbor, Maya, alive.

ACKNOWLEDGEMENTS

Thanks to the editors of the following publications where some of the poems in this collection first appeared:

2River: "Potatoes," "The Path"
Atticus Review: "'Barb's Healing Hands'"
Cascadia Review: "Icebergs Near Twillingate," "Presence," "Ancestry" (retitled here as "Immigrants")
Chariton Review: "Pine Siskin"
Hinchas de Poesia: "Bat in Daylight," "Coming to Terms with the Fact that I May Never Get the Hang of Mississippi John Hurt's 'Monday Morning Blues,'" "Swing"
Miramar: "Ax," "Meadowlark," "The Return"
Mudlark: "Honeymoon"
Rat's Ass Review: "America, Great Once Again"
Raven Chronicles: "Great Apes at the Zoo," "Neighborhood Crows"
Split Lip Magazine: "Ash"
Terrain.org: "Union Creek in Winter," "Spoon," "View of Richmond Beach." "Tying a Tie" and "Airborne" won the *Terrain.org* 8th Annual Contest for poetry.

The following poems first appeared in *Ice Children*, a chapbook published by Split Lip Press, 2014: "Catching the Vase," "Dahlias," "The Gods," "Ice Children of the Andes," "My Father Mows the Lawn," "The Unfocused Eyes of Drones"

To his everlasting regret, Edward Harkness did not see Elvis when the King of Rock 'n' Roll visited Seattle during the World's Fair in 1962. Other than that, Harkness is a happy husband to Linda, father to Ned and Devin, and grandfather to Clio. Having retired after a 30+ year career as a writing teacher at Shoreline Community College, he now devotes his time to other pleasures: gardening, cycling, visiting the kids and, now and then, making poems. He is the author of two full-length poetry collections, *Saying the Necessary* and *Beautiful Passing Lives,* both from Pleasure Boat Studio press. His most recent chapbook, *Ice Children,* was published by Split Lip Press in 2014. Two poems in this collection, "Tying a Tie" and "Airborne," won the Terrain.org annual poetry prize for 2017. He lives in Shoreline, Washington, about a mile from the north Seattle home where he grew up, and where his mother, Doris Harkness, whose art works grace the covers of this book, still lives.

CPSIA information can be obtained
at www.ICGtesting.com
Printed in the USA
LVHW09s0046160918
590261LV00003B/486/P